REAL TALK
ABOUT
SHOWING UP,
SCREWING UP
AND TRYING
AGAIN

BEING AN
ALLY

EDITED BY
SHAKIRAH BOURNE
& DANA ALISON LEVY

FEATURING ESSAYS BY
DERICK BROOKS, SHAKIRAH
BOURNE, NAOMI AND NATALIE
EVANS, LIZZIE HUXLEY-JONES,
DANA ALISON LEVY, AND A.J. SASS

This edition first published in Great Britain in 2023 by
Dorling Kindersley Limited
DK, One Embassy Gardens, 8 Viaduct Gardens,
London SW11 7BW

Contains content previously published in
Allies: Real Talk About Showing Up, Screwing Up, and Trying Again (2021)

The authorised representative in the EEA is
Dorling Kindersley Verlag GmbH. Arnulfstr. 124,
80636 Munich, Germany

Page and cover design copyright © 2021, 2023 Dorling Kindersley Limited
A Penguin Random House Company

"Dana's Absolutely Perfect Fail-Safe No Mistakes Guaranteed Way to Be an Ally"
Text copyright © Dana Alison Levy, 2021
"Dismantling Judgement" Text copyright © Lizzie Huxley-Jones, 2021
"Travel Logs of a Black Caribbean Woman: Embracing the Glitches"
Text copyright © Shakirah Bourne, 2021
"Stutter Buddy" Text and Illustration copyright © Derick Brooks, 2021
"This Is What It Feels Like" Text copyright © Andrew Sass, 2021
"Why Didn't Anyone Else Say Anything?" Text copyright © Naomi Evans and Natalie Evans, 2021

The moral rights of the authors and illustrator have been asserted.

10 9 8 7 6 5 4 3 2 1
001–335606–Feb/2023

This book is substantially a work of nonfiction based on the experiences and
recollections of the authors. In some cases names of people, places, dates, sequences,
or the detail of events have been changed to protect the privacy of others.

Cover design by Anita Mangan

A CIP catalogue record for this book
is available from the British Library.
ISBN: 978-0-2416-1925-4

Printed and bound in China

For the curious
www.dk.com

MIX
Paper | Supporting
responsible forestry
FSC™ C018179

This book was made with Forest
Stewardship Council ™ certified
paper – one small step in DK's
commitment to a sustainable future.
**For more information go to
www.dk.com/our-green-pledge**

WAIT!

We're so glad you're here, and we wanted to share
some important information with you before you read on. Each of the
personal essays in this book explores experiences about real things
that happened to real people. Some of them cover topics that could
make you feel anxious or upset. These experiences might remind you
of things you've been through, or things that people you care about
have been through. It's okay to put the book down, clear your head,
and come back whenever you feel ready to read some more.

DANA'S ABSOLUTELY PERFECT FAIL-SAFE NO MISTAKES GUARANTEED WAY TO BE AN ALLY

DANA ALISON LEVY

Hahahahaha! That's so . . . oh. Wait. You thought I was serious with that title?

Yeah, sorry about that.

Being a good ally without making mistakes is like eating popcorn without dropping any on the floor: it's possible, but let's be honest, it rarely happens.

For instance, let's try this quiz:

1. You (an able-bodied person) see someone in a wheelchair moving through a doorway. Should you:

    a. Rush to open the door for them

    b. Leave them alone

c. Ask them if they want help

d. It's complicated

2. You (a white person) want to show support for a Black Lives Matter protest so you:

   a. Post on social media

   b. Attend a protest

   c. Write a letter to your local paper

   d. Do nothing: it's performative and you don't want to co-opt spaces for Black voices

   e. It's complicated

3. On social media an old friend you haven't talked to in years posts a cruel meme that disrespects transgender people. Creeping around her other posts, you see a lot of problematic content. Do you:

   a. Call her out and put her on blast

   b. Unfriend her

   c. Write a long passionate DM about why her stuff is a mess

   d. It's complicated

YOU GUESSED IT. BEING AN ALLY IS COMPLICATED. AND I CERTAINLY DON'T HAVE ALL THE ANSWERS. I HAVE SCREWED UP MORE TIMES THAN I CAN COUNT, AND IT FEELS GROSS EVERY TIME.

You guessed it. Being an ally is complicated. And I certainly don't have all the answers. I have screwed up more times than I can count, and it feels gross every time. I get nervous when I'm going to speak up or get involved, even after years of practice. But I still try.

But let's back up.

What do we even mean when we talk about being an ally? We can at least all agree on that, right?

Well, wrong, because there are lots of different ways of defining it and, more importantly, acting on that definition.

But here's a place to start.

BEING AN ALLY, FIRST OF ALL, IS A CONSTANT ACT – NOT A STATE OF BEING.

Being an ally, first of all, is a constant act – not a state of being. You can be a wonderful ally in one situation and completely fail to act in another. It's not a level to reach in a game (Achievement unlocked! Level Ally! Upgrade your gems! That would be cool, but sadly, no). Being an ally is about someone other than yourself, and it's about supporting those others . . . whether or not you know them, whether or not they are aware you're supporting them, whether or not you have any personal connection.

One of the trickiest parts of being an ally is that no one is just one thing. The idea of intersectionality is where it really gets funky. Intersectionality means that no one is defined by just one element of themselves, and these different elements intersect and can even contradict.

So for instance: I am a woman, and I'm Jewish, two elements of my identity that, in our society, can elicit cruelty, ignorance, danger, and prejudice. However I am white, I am able-bodied, I'm middle class; all aspects of my identity that give me privilege. So in some situations I might be vulnerable, and in others, I have significantly more power than others in the room.

It's confusing, right?

If you're Black and wealthy and able-bodied; if you're white and queer and disabled; if you're Asian and visually impaired and female; if you're transgender and Latinx and famous . . . do you need an ally? Should you be showing up as an ally? Who "deserves" (and wow, there's a loaded word!) our allyship? Who can make the perfect judgement call to tell the rest of the world what's right and wrong?

Say it with me, loud for the folks at the back:

IT'S COMPLICATED.

It's even complicated to know what to call it. The term ally has become a common way to talk about the responsibilities we have to show up and support each other, and in particular for those with privilege to show up and support people and communities that are systemically oppressed. But not everyone thinks it's a great word. Some argue that too many people claim the label without doing the work. Others say it doesn't go far enough, and that allies might empathize with and support individuals, but they aren't doing the hard, sometimes dangerous work of breaking down oppressive systems. There are those who say we need accomplices, not allies, to really make change.

Did I mention it's complicated??

Here's one thing I know: these are good, important conversations about labels and what they mean. But we should not let the complexity of the word distract us from the urgency of the work. Whatever we call ourselves – an ally, an accomplice, a

> **WHATEVER WE CALL OURSELVES – AN ALLY, AN ACCOMPLICE, A CO-CONSPIRATOR – WE MUST DO BETTER TO UNDERSTAND, EMPATHIZE, AND TAKE ACTION TO CARE FOR EACH OTHER.**

co-conspirator – we must do better to understand, empathize, and take action to care for each other.

Being an ally is not about your personal growth (though that's likely going to happen), or about diversifying your friendships (though that will likely happen, too). It's not about having all the answers to school those non-allies in everything they're doing wrong. Being an ally means that when you screw up (and you will), you apologize and do better . . . but you don't insist on forgiveness, or try to make the other person process it with you, or beat yourself up so badly that it suddenly becomes their job to reassure you!

So what is it? What is allyship?

It's continuously showing up and using the power you have – by speaking out, by physically using your body, by educating yourself, by using your resources (financial and otherwise), and by amplifying marginalized voices – in support of those who have less power due to ongoing systemic racism, ableism, sexism, religious persecution, and other forms of oppression.

There are a lot of definitions of being an ally, but one of my favourites comes from Dr Laura Jiménez, an educator and advocate. On her *BookToss* blog, she has a shirt that reads: "ALLY: [noun/verb] To cause a ruckus and pass the mic."

I LOVE THIS DEFINITION.

Because as an ally, sometimes you have to make some noise, and sometimes you have to get out of the way and let others speak for themselves. And figuring out when to act and when to stay quiet is a constant learning process.

Allyship looks different depending on who you are and what stage of life you're in. An adult has different tools available than a teen. A celebrity with ten million social media followers has different tools than a college student. A bazillionaire philanthropist has different tools than me. But we all have power. And a dozen times a day we make decisions, large and small, on how we will use it.

The way we use our power depends on our strengths, our tools, and our comfort level. I'm going to talk about some of the quieter ways we can be allies . . . not because I don't think that sometimes we need to raise a ruckus, but because I'm better at the quiet stuff. I'm still working my way up to ruckus status.

So let's talk about some of the tools.

QUIET ALLYSHIP

Being an ally sometimes means quietly changing your habits in ways that others may never notice. Like what? You ask. How about:

- ▶ Buy your stuff – books, shoes, coffee, cupcakes – from BIPOC-owned businesses, locally or online

- ▶ Read books by diverse authors, and then hype them up to your friends

- ▶ Follow diverse voices on social media, especially local ones and folks without millions of followers. Amplify them and help them get noticed

- ▶ Educate yourself. Which Indigenous peoples might

have lived on the land where you live now? What other versions of history offer different perspectives than what you're reading in school?

▶ Share your pronouns, and normalize asking or being asked, so that gender fluid, non-binary, and transgender folks don't have the full burden of educating people

These are all ways of being an ally that don't require a lot of bravery or practice, and again, it's not something you'll do for a while then move on to Stage Two. This is lifelong work . . . we vote with our wallets and our time way more often than we ever get to vote in elections, so get in the habit of practising allyship in small ways every day!

For me this means that when I give books as gifts – and I give a lot of books! It's kind of my thing – I almost always give books by diverse authors, usually focusing on new writers or those whose

> **THIS IS LIFELONG WORK . . . WE VOTE WITH OUR WALLETS AND OUR TIME WAY MORE OFTEN THAN WE EVER GET TO VOTE IN ELECTIONS, SO GET IN THE HABIT OF PRACTISING ALLYSHIP IN SMALL WAYS EVERY DAY!**

books aren't huge bestsellers. It means that I pay attention to a lot of incredibly smart people on social media who don't follow me back and never will, because I'm grateful to absorb their wisdom. It means I read more nonfiction than I used to, trying to fill the gaps in my knowledge left by a white supremacist education system.

And being a quiet ally also sometimes means just that – keeping quiet.

Remember when I said that it's not about you? Yeah, it's really not about you.

You, my dear ally-in-training, are going to be learning and processing and unlearning all through this journey! It's hard and it's tiring, and you definitely need friends to talk to. You might need a sympathetic shoulder to lean on. There might be a time you did something you're proud of, and you want to talk about it. You may even complain about how you tried to do the right thing but it backfired. Totally fair!

HOWEVER.

Do not drop that load of learning and missteps on the people you are trying to support! And that includes your friends! If you have a wonderful circle of diverse friends and you tried to be an ally and screwed up (Again! It's gonna happen. Get comfortable with it), the person to go to for tea and sympathy and a debrief is NOT your Black Friend or your Muslim Friend or your Disabled Friend or whatever friend of the same marginalization as the one you were defending. They are aware of the cruelty directed towards their communities – they don't need you to tell them all about it.

Part of the work of being an ally is taking that processing elsewhere, and sparing them the burden of your questions and guilt.

Yet another way of being a quiet ally is recognizing that sometimes you need to step back. Let's say you, a white person and ally, are at a local Black Lives Matter protest, and the newspaper reporter comes over to ask you about it. All around you are other protesters, many of whom are Black. Do you talk to the reporter, share all your outrage, and drop some hard facts around police violence? Or do you step away and urge them to talk to one of the Black protesters?

Like that quiz in the beginning . . . it's complicated. (For example, not everyone wants to be quoted in the newspaper; not everyone feels safe). But being a good ally often means NOT speaking up when there are folks who can speak for themselves.

I have had to consider this kind of allyship a lot lately. I'm a white woman who writes books for kids. There are a lot of us. There are a rather embarrassing number more white authors than BIPOC authors. And far too often at multi-author events, at conferences, book festivals, bookstores, and so on, I would sit with five or six other authors, and we were all white.

Not acceptable.

So I, and many others, made a pledge a few years ago: no more all-white panels. No more all-white conferences. No more token author of colour amidst a sea of whiteness.

What that means is that when I get invited to a book event – and let me just say, it's not like they're beating down the door! I don't get a lot of these invitations, and it's always exciting when I do – but when I get invited, I ask the awkward question. I send an email thanking them, then say "I have taken a pledge to no longer participate in all-white book events. Can you tell me who else is invited and what other authors have committed to being there?" Or I might say "Thank you for inviting me to be on this panel. I've taken a pledge not to participate in all-white book events, so can I suggest you ask XX or YY to join instead?"

I often wind up declining the event. Sometimes the event organizers tell me they've invited certain BIPOC authors, but those authors declined. Sometimes they give a metaphorical shrug, like they did the best they could. Sometimes they're genuinely horrified when they realize their bias and are grateful for the insight. They promise to do better the following year. And often they do improve . . . but they don't always invite me back.

And I get it – the organizers are often volunteers, the events are often poorly paid, and like I said, there are way more white authors than BIPOC authors.

But it's not good enough. So I won't go. And I don't get cookies, and I don't get thanked, and if I'm being totally honest, I don't even get a glow of satisfaction. Sometimes I have FOMO and wish I had done the damn event, because I'm human and don't like missing out. And I'm not telling you now so YOU can give me cookies or tell me what a wonderful ally I am!

I'm sharing it because how can we know how to help if no one shows us? How can we use our power until someone points out that we have some?

Here's one final thought on being a quiet ally: consider calling in people in your circles who are using problematic language or sharing misinformation. Unless you live under a rock (and if you do, is it warm and cosy and can I join you?), you have probably heard about "Call-Out Culture" and "Cancel Culture". There is a tension between people being held accountable for their choices, and a kind of feeding frenzy of disapproval that can make the punishment outweigh the crime. This is a whole complicated mess of a subject, and it would take another essay

and several packages of cookies for me to even attempt to unpack it. But in short, it's the idea that the only way to get people to change is to publicly shame them.

And let me be clear: sometimes people need to be called out. Sometimes people with a lot of power – politicians, celebrities, even famous authors – say things that are unacceptably racist or prejudiced. And sometimes they do not step back when someone tries to explain the problem, but instead double down on their misbelief. And yes, in these cases, calling them out and holding them accountable, and seeking to educate the general public about their views, is justified and necessary.

But calling in is also a useful tool, and often can be tried before trying to shame someone into enlightenment. Calling in is when someone genuinely might not know that their statements are hurtful. Calling in offers someone a bridge back from their mistake, and is done with an assumption of good faith. It's saying: "You might not have known this, so I am telling you. And now that you know, you can do better."

Calling in is one way to be an ally, to make it clear that certain language or behaviour isn't okay, without going to the nuclear option of publicly shaming someone. Here's an example: until fairly recently I did not realize there was anything problematic about the phrase "spirit animal". I had heard it used as a pop culture reference ("Taylor Swift is my spirit animal; Narwhals are my spirit animal") and thought it was clever and kind of funny.

Until I read how, as a very real part of Native American Indigenous traditions, this co-opting and joking version is totally disrespectful.

But it's just a joke, right?

But no one was trying to be offensive, right?

> **CALLING IN OFFERS SOMEONE A BRIDGE BACK FROM THEIR MISTAKE, AND IS DONE WITH AN ASSUMPTION OF GOOD FAITH. IT'S SAYING: "YOU MIGHT NOT HAVE KNOWN THIS, SO I AM TELLING YOU. AND NOW THAT YOU KNOW, YOU CAN DO BETTER."**

But obviously we aren't serious, right?

Yeah. Wrong.

So now I have this knowledge, and I have it because I've read several different Native American authors' views on the subject. And yet people I know, who are generally aware and careful and – yes, good allies – are still using this phrase.

So I call them in. I don't retweet them or tag them in a social media post shaming them for the problematic language. I send a private message, saying "hey, this is something I learnt recently, and here's a link to learn more, but the phrase 'spirit animal' is really problematic and you might want to change it."

I call people in a lot. Depending on the issue and how well I know them, it might be really uncomfortable or no big deal. I will not tell you how long I spend crafting a three-sentence private message sometimes, because it's embarrassing and probably explains why I keep missing work deadlines. But often when I take the time to do this, people are grateful.

Of course, not always. Remember earlier, when I talked about all us white authors flooding events? After I had signed the pledge, I reached out to another (white woman) author friend. I explained why I wasn't going to an upcoming event, and asked her if she would also commit to the pledge: if she would refuse to attend all-white author events.

She refused.

HOW CAN I BE SURE I HAVEN'T SCREWED THIS UP??

I explained my reasoning, shared the importance of representation, and offered up some statistics on publishing.* She still refused, saying she understood the issue but she had to think of her own book sales, and wasn't willing to miss out on opportunities in this way.

And that was the end of it. I didn't call her out. I didn't put her on blast. But I quietly changed my own calculus about whether I'd promote her books or give them as gifts or invite her to events. It wasn't a situation where I had a lot of power, but I used what I had.

And that's really what being a quiet ally means. It means recognizing the small bits of power everyone has – to buy things, to listen to things, to talk about things with friends and family – and being intentional in how we use them. You can probably think of ten more examples. You might be doing them right now. AWESOME. Keep doing them. You don't get a prize, or a cookie, but that doesn't mean it's not vitally important.

I'll be honest: writing this essay is really hard. I am balancing on a skinny ledge, arms windmilling frantically, hoping I don't fall down on either side. I don't feel like I know nearly enough to tell anyone else how to be an ally: SLAM! I fall over on the Impostor Syndrome side. I don't want to brag and claim space that others should have: CRASH! I fall the other way on the Centring Myself side. How can I be sure I haven't screwed this up??

That one's easy. I can't. I can't be sure. I might screw this up.

But I still have to try.

Am I raising a ruckus? Maybe not. Am I going to keep showing up, as best I can?

You'd better believe it.

Last quiz question:

4. You want to be an ally but you're afraid you don't know enough and you'll screw up. Should you:

    a. Read books and blogs, listen to podcasts, and follow activists and advocates on social media?

    b. Speak up to friends, family, classmates, and others when you hear something racist or oppressive?

    c. Find friends who are not part of marginalized groups who can support you while you figure out this ally stuff?

    d. Examine your own mistakes and learn from them but don't beat yourself up?

    e. It's complicated, but yeah, all of the above?

You know the answer, and so do I. So let's get back to work.

---

*Quick synopsis of the publishing statistics: they're dismal and almost all published kids' books are written by white authors. For more specifics, look at the Center for Diversity in Children's Literature's study.

DISMANTLING JUDGEMENT

LIZZIE HUXLEY-JONES

I've had many seizures in public.

One time, I crossed a busy London road with my partner Tim, only to keel over as my feet hit the pavement on the other side. A passerby whipped the coats off her children as well as her own, placing them around my body like a shield against the world.

Another time, I stumbled bleary-eyed out of a movie theatre, having witnessed a particularly flashy scene there had been no warnings about. Everything went black, but as I began to wake up, my ears filled with jauntily played horns and drums. Circus music promoting a film I can no longer remember. The sparkling star pattern of the faux marble floor reflected on the lobby ceiling.

Those are some of the many times my partner has been there for and, crucially, are the ones people could see.

We call disabilities that are not easily visible "invisible disabilities". To the untrained eye a person might look completely fine, but may be struggling with a mental, physical, or neurological condition that impacts how they process, move, and interact with the world. This can make accessing support and asking for help much more difficult.

When you have a brain like mine, one that is prone to short-circuiting in hidden ways, navigating the world can be a difficult, sometimes dangerous, experience.

The year before the COVID-19 pandemic, I developed an orange-size cyst on my right ovary that kept bursting thanks to untreated endometriosis – we affectionately named him Drippy. Managing pain took over my life, even more than it had before, and I mostly stayed home, grasping little moments of independence when I had energy, while we waited six months for a surgery to sort everything out.

> **WHEN YOU HAVE A BRAIN LIKE MINE, ONE THAT IS PRONE TO SHORT-CIRCUITING IN HIDDEN WAYS, NAVIGATING THE WORLD CAN BE A DIFFICULT, SOMETIMES DANGEROUS, EXPERIENCE.**

Just before Drippy's arrival, a special interest in musical theatre had unleashed itself with full force. This meant I had been sitting on an unsated desire to see a really good showstopping number with the West End only a twenty-minute train ride from my house, and limited at-home outlets to distract me from mounting an expedition. With support from my friends and Tim, I had managed to see *Come From Away* in September, and I had tickets to see *Dear Evan Hansen* in November when it opened in London. While I wouldn't rank *Evan* as a favourite musical, "Waving Through a Window" had become a bit of an anthem for me. I would belt it out as I hobbled around my tiny flat, clutching onto my protruding belly like a heavily pregnant person. I was told in October that my surgery would be happening in November, and the possibility of not being able to go made me want to go even more.

Luckily, my surgery was scheduled for after the night we had tickets, so I was all clear to go have a fun night out with my friend Lauren. That morning, I felt a bit strange – a little off-colour in a way I couldn't work out – but as this ranked fairly low compared to the myriad ways I'd felt for six months, I decided to go. I left the house armoured in an enormous fluffy pink coat and luminous yellow checked dress, channelling Cher Horowitz energy.

We had a really nice time, and I cried my eyes out – because I will always cry at any piece of slightly emotive theatre. It was only as I boarded the train at London Bridge that a familiar strangeness hit me. A seizure was coming.

I have two main types of seizure. One is essentially a jazzed-up faint and looks like a classic convulsion, the kind I had in those stories at the beginning. If not enough blood is getting to my head or I'm too hot, down I go. Over time, these have gotten easier to manage – you'll never see me without a huge bottle of water and an emergency salty snack pack.

The other is a kind of absence, heralded by a collection of odd sensations that we call an aura (which, a little confusingly, is technically a conscious seizure of its own). I will smell smoke that's not there, my teeth and jaw ache, and my body feels like it's rising, like I'm on a roller coaster going down the big drop. My neurologist and I think they're linked to how my autistic wiring processes overstimulation and stress, which makes them tricky to predict and prevent. My partner says that I look like I've powered down, and in a sense I have – I often don't know they've happened, the only sign being my little dog sitting in my lap,

licking my face as I come round. But as I get closer to my brain rebooting like an ancient PC, I get clumsy and my words slur. I look drunk. And when the seizure is over, sometimes I can't speak at all.

Imaginary smoke filled the air around me and my heart started racing, thick heavy palpitations that I could hear in my ears. I slipped out of my coat, worried that I was unknowingly overheating, as autism means I lack interoception, the body's sixth sense, so can never tell if I'm too hot or cold. My fingers fumbled over my phone screen, writing "I feel strange" over to Tim, trying to remember how to tell him what was happening through the panic. What if this was a convulsion? What if my cyst burst again? What if I missed my stop?

A few years ago, I would go wandering, unknowingly having a seizure the whole time. My brain would usually autopilot me to safety and I would wake up in cafés or bookstores. My train was halfway to my home station. I had to hold on for another ten minutes. If I didn't, I'd miss my stop, ending up at the airport or the seaside where the train terminated.

Tim tried to keep me present by telling me about the new headphones he'd bought, but the nausea started to set in. My tongue felt huge in my mouth, an alien body part. I started to cry as my head twitched. This was definitely an aura. Blackout was getting closer.

I took a deep breath. Stay awake, I begged, running my fingers through my furry coat. My terrified reflection mirrored on the window, lit against the darkness outside. I tried to speak, but the swollen tongue that both was and wasn't mine wouldn't obey. A small moan poured out of me, words collapsed into a slick of noise, and I began to cry harder.

Another breath. I looked down at my phone, and pulled up the

THE LOOK IS AN ACT OF JUDGEMENT, WHEN WHAT YOU'RE SEEING DOESN'T MATCH UP WITH YOUR EXPECTATIONS, OR EXPERIENCE TELLS YOU SOMETHING STRANGE IS HAPPENING. IT HAPPENS WHEN PEOPLE ARE UNEQUIPPED, NERVOUS, OR UNFAMILIAR WITH A RANGE OF EXPERIENCES.

notes app. If I could catch someone's attention, I could show them a note on there that would explain I needed help. There weren't many people in the carriage around me. After wiping away tears and possible eyeliner trails, I turned my head to each of them in turn, hoping desperately to catch their eye. I did, a few times. And they all either looked away, or gave me The Look.

I find both reading and recognizing faces quite difficult – I've mistaken perfect strangers for my best friends just because they shared similar approximate outlines – but I know The Look a mile off. It's the moment that a person looks at you, sees something they think is strange, and so turn themselves away. It lightning-flashes over their features, and then they are gone before I can protest.

I've been seeing The Look since I was a child. At tweenage sleepovers where I couldn't handle the noise and asked if I could call my mum and go home. At a nice pub when, gathered with a lot of new people plus an ex, my arm wouldn't stop tremoring and these relative strangers kept glancing at me as I held tight onto my wrist, willing my body to stop rebelling. The Look is an act of judgement, when what you're seeing doesn't match up with your expectations, or experience tells you something strange is happening. It happens when people are unequipped, nervous, or unfamiliar with a range of experiences.

I needed help that day on the train. I was scared. I just needed someone to reach out and ask if I was okay. But they didn't. Somehow, I managed to stumble off the train at my stop with all my things, and waited in the ice-cold air for Tim to find me on the platform. No one there asked if I was okay either.

You might be surprised by this, but I don't blame people for The Look, or for their inaction. I know that people took one look at my outfit, my tears, and the phone clutched in my hand and thought either that I was too drunk or just-dumped or just a "hysterical woman". This makes me a little sad because I think even if I was any of the above, I still deserved compassion from strangers. The point is, I suppose, that they didn't see a disabled person who needed help.

The difference between this seizure and the ones in the movie theatre or on the street is that people knew what to do then. When I convulse or collapse, people come running. They might not know much about seizures, but they know to cushion my head, and maybe call an ambulance.

Hospital TV shows love to have a seizure around the point the patient gets really ill – *House* in particular loved throwing this out three-quarters through an episode – so people recognize that convulsions mean someone is in trouble. When I have an absence seizure people don't connect me blankly staring like a rabbit in the headlights with a neurological disorder. This is where The Look comes in – being unequipped to recognize that what is happening to me is a medical issue, that I might be a vulnerable person in need of help.

I learnt a saying recently from editor Dana: "you don't know until you know." As an eternal optimist, I like to think that people are generally good. The Look and inaction come from being unequipped; undereducated about the full swathe of disability experiences; or just not knowing how to help, worried about making things worse. That goes for how best to comfort a crying fluff ball as well as being able to recognize that my miscellaneous odd behaviours meant something serious was happening. It's ignorance, not malice. And so, I don't feel anger towards those people who didn't help. I just wish I could revisit them like a friendly Ghost of Christmas Past and tell them how I experienced that interaction, or lack thereof, so they could learn.

I grew up in a pretty atypical family. I wasn't diagnosed as autistic or with Hypermobile Ehlers-Danlos Syndrome (hEDS) until I was in my late twenties, but I showed all the hallmarks of both from a young age. My parents and sister are all invisibly disabled, the only hints of difference seen in a reaction to flashing lights, or the way they use a golf umbrella like a walking stick. My grandparents, aunts and uncles, and other miscellaneous relatives were also predominantly disabled people – that's a good batch of genetics for you.

Disability was, and is, the norm for me. My childhood memories are peppered with mundane, vaguely medical moments – helping stretch my dad's back to free his sciatic nerve, putting my sister in recovery position, and helping my mum reach things. Our bungalow wasn't a hospital by any stretch – it was a home, and these were all part of our day. Adjusting plans last minute, checking if someone needs help to do a task, learning the warning signs that they're struggling, accepting that today is just not a leave-the-house kind of day, and knowing that their pain can change in a moment are important ways to support disabled people, and are just part of my coming-of-age story. Admittedly, I think having this kind of relaxed-compassion to life made it much easier for me to cope with the changes to my body as I eventually became more disabled as an adult.

Invisible disabilities aren't so much invisible to me as quiet. I can catch them in the way someone stands with the weight on one hip, and know they're hypermobile – I like to say people with hEDS stand like a late-stage Jenga game. The way someone flaps their hands, wrings their clothes through their fingers, or taps out of a hug like my Nanna used to. The deep, bone-rattling sigh they make when they get onto the bus and see there are no seats.

On days when I'm out in London and feeling well, I look for these quiet signs. When I first moved to London, frustrated by the lack of support for people who need seats on the tube, I would eagle eye everyone boarding the train for a different kind of look – a weariness, a desperate burn in the eyes, the look that says "I need to ask for help, but I don't know how to." If I saw it and could stand, I'd jump out of my seat, asking if they would like it. The flash of relief and gratitude is one I've seen on my own face, reflected in the glassed darkness when someone does the same for me.

> **INVISIBLE DISABILITIES AREN'T SO MUCH INVISIBLE TO ME AS QUIET.**

I was just one of the many people involved in campaigning for a Please Offer Me a Seat badge for the London transportation network, arguing that it meant people didn't need to be fluent in other people's pain; they just needed to look for the badge. I also quietly hoped that people would start to associate the badge with that tired desperation, and would learn to see it on its own, building up their compassion for fellow passengers.

All this experience and trying doesn't make me perfect. I still miss things, but I keep my eyes open, listen, and learn. If in doubt, I offer help – the embarrassment of an affronted stranger is better than leaving someone struggling. I'm actively trying to unlearn judgements that have snuck in without me realizing, which often contradict what I actually think.

I do think that the normalization of disability in my upbringing, on top of my own experiences, has attuned me to others' quiet needs. Essentially, it's familiarity. It's a combination of preexisting knowledge and knowing to listen where I lack it. It's what the people wearing The Look were lacking.

So, what can you do to dismantle that instinctive judgement and grow your compassion if you didn't grow up surrounded by disabled people?

The very first thing you should do, as with any marginalization you don't share, is to accept that you probably know less about their experiences than you think you do. Not only do you not have firsthand experience of their life, but the media we consume – books, film, television, the news, and even charity communications – are usually filtered through an abled lens.

> YOU'RE NOT EXPECTED TO BECOME AN EXPERT AND THERE DEFINITELY WON'T BE A TEST, BUT IT'S GOOD TO UNDERSTAND WHAT PEOPLE AROUND YOU MIGHT BE GOING THROUGH, SO YOU CAN SUPPORT THEM.

Autism, for example, tends to be told by the carers, parents, siblings; this is why I edited *Stim*, an anthology of autistic people's writing – because everything I read was about us, not by us. This is replicated in many fields of disability, and means that historically our individual voices have been boosted less.

Second, start listening. This is potentially a huge project considering just how many disabilities there are, but think about the disabled people in your life, your school, your workplace, those you follow online. Listen to what they say about their experiences, and believe them. You're not expected to become an expert and there definitely won't be a test, but it's good to understand what people around you might be going through, so you can support them. There will be things that make no logical sense, but you are not their doctor nor in their body, so bite down that urge to question.

Our media constantly tells stories of people faking their disability, especially the news that reports every sensationalist story of benefits fraud – particularly where a claimed disability is involved – even though the rate of fraud, which is reported combined with error on their part, is usually less than 1%. In the UK, this has emboldened people to report on their neighbours who they suspect of fraud, which results in an immediate freeze in their money that can last weeks, even if there's no evidence of fraud.

Even I as a disabled person cannot explain why some days I can walk with limited pain, and others, like the day before I wrote this paragraph, it took me six hours to be able to sit upright. Ambulatory wheelchair users know this feeling particularly well, often being interrogated by perfect strangers about whether they are faking their disability.

I don't currently use a wheelchair day-to-day, but when I visited Disneyland Paris with my friends, getting up out of the wheelchair to walk to the toilets definitely earned me a few of

The Looks from people who couldn't match up the two mes: the disabled wheelchair occupying me, and the walking me. Somewhat ironically, during the same trip but on a day when I wasn't using a wheelchair, a woman also in the disabled entrance to *Mickey's Christmas Big Band* remarked that they must be letting anyone in, implying that I wasn't disabled. Luckily my ferocious best friend leapt to my defence, and I hope that woman learnt something from it. The people in the toilets couldn't match me visibly using a mobility aid but being ambulatory with being disabled, while the woman in the queue couldn't equate disability with me standing without one. Sometimes it feels like you can't win! Living with a fluctuating disability is like living in a world of contradiction, and the best thing in my experience is for those around me to graciously adapt to my today.

It's worth saying that The Looks are not confined to train carriages and Disneyland Paris. One of the biggest problems disabled people face is disbelief from some medical professionals, which can leave us without care and support, which can make our disabilities worse and absolutely tanks our mental health. This is why it took me the best part of twenty-five years to get diagnosed as autistic, twenty years for Hypermobile Ehlers-Danlos syndrome, eighteen for endometriosis, ten years to recognize one type of my seizures were related to my blood pressure. Time and again I would ask doctors for help with chronic pain, periods that meant I blacked out, or the anxiety I felt having to get onto a commuter train, only for them to ignore what I was saying, instead tuning into their presumptions.

Many doctors have a habit of seeing a person with a list of problems as being a hypochondriac, as opposed to someone who might have a genetic predisposition that links them all together. I started pushing back against my misdiagnoses around the time I tried to access an autism diagnosis and was sent to a child psychiatrist, despite being in my late twenties.

I was fed up with hearing doctors tell me their preconceptions rather than anything that matched my experiences, but that's truly, truly exhausting. I was only able to do it because my partner had my back and because, to be frank with you, I'd decided enough was enough.

The thing you need to understand is that my experience isn't unique; most of my friends with invisible disabilities have similar stories, especially fat people who are always told to "just lose weight" no matter their condition.

Again, you are not expected to become an expert in all this, or launch the campaign for better disability training for medical staff (although if the fancy takes you, I certainly won't stop you); the thing you should do is empathize. Don't imply the doctor just didn't understand, or that perhaps we didn't phrase things right; this just adds to the medical trauma that many of us carry. Listen to, learn from, and support us.

The third point is, in my opinion, the one that requires the most work. It's about practising catching your judgemental brain making an assumption, and interrogating it. And by this I don't just mean the obviously negative thoughts, but any thought you might have about what a particular disabled person might experience. Recognize it. Sit with it. Ask yourself where you learnt this information. Was it from a disabled person, or from a movie, or something your parents said? How long ago did you hear it? Does it match up with what the people you have listened to say? Do you need to go and learn more? This process can be uncomfortable, but it's important work, and core to being an ally to disabled people.

In practising all these tools and expanding your compassion, you will be well on the way to both dismantling your judgement and being a great ally to disabled people.

3

TRAVEL LOGS OF A BLACK CARIBBEAN WOMAN: EMBRACING THE GLITCHES

SHAKIRAH BOURNE

In *The Matrix* movie, Neo is looking for answers because he has a niggling feeling that something is wrong with his world. He experiences "Glitches" – inexplicable errors in his reality. When he gets a message to "follow the white rabbit", he meets Morpheus, who gives him the choice to see the ugly truth, and Neo discovers he's been living in a simulated reality controlled by machines.

Morpheus was Black. Neo was white. And though race relations weren't relevant to the plot of the film, when Morpheus gives Neo the chance to remain ignorant of the realities of the world and keep his rose-tinted perspective of life, his privilege was clear – he got to choose.

So many people of colour do not.

A key step to becoming an ally is empathy – opening your eyes to the reality of the less privileged and acknowledging that despite your best efforts, you may have implicit biases and prejudices.

These are travel logs of my physical and psychological journey to recognizing racism underneath the veil of pretence. A round trip from ignorance to awareness.

In the movie, when Neo moved towards implementing change, he encountered Agents, guardians of the matrix who defended the system against anyone who threatened to reveal the truth.

Beware, the agents that protect systemic racism in the real world may be operated by your sweet old neighbour who bakes you cookies, a beloved family member, or your closest friend.

And allies can be those who you least expect . . .

A KEY STEP TO BECOMING AN ALLY IS EMPATHY – OPENING YOUR EYES TO THE REALITY OF THE LESS PRIVILEGED AND ACKNOWLEDGING THAT DESPITE YOUR BEST EFFORTS, YOU MAY HAVE IMPLICIT BIASES AND PREJUDICES.

BARBADOS

To an outsider, Barbados is a picture of racial harmony. A place to holiday. Take long walks on white sand and have smiling locals serve you food and drink on the beach.

"Happy" is our brand.

People of all races greet each other on the street, mingle at restaurants, and apologize with a chuckle when our shopping trollies accidentally bump in supermarket aisles.

A photographer could snap a photo at any minute and use it in a brochure.

Early on, someone tried to shatter my virtual reality. They told me Barbados is like a successful apartheid. Everyone lives in relative peace with each other, maintaining our matrix – our fragile dream world of civility. That there is no need for "Whites Only" signs to separate us. Everyone knows their place.

I dismissed that theory. Made excuses. I didn't want to disturb my bubble. Until I experienced my first Glitch.

BARBADOS, 1997

I was devastated when I found out I had gotten into one of the most prestigious secondary schools on the island. You see, I had heard stories about snobby rich students who ate sandwiches with knives and forks and turned their noses up at everything fun. I came from a poor family and thought I would be a fish out of water, a prime candidate for shunning.

It was a relief to discover this was not the case. Yes, most of my new classmates came from middle and upper class families, but we were all scared eleven-year-olds in new blue tunics and white-starched blouses, anxious about the new environment and desperate to make friends.

For the first time, I had white classmates. But though there had been no white kids at my primary school in a working class community, I was no stranger to interacting with white people.

My mother was a waitress at a hotel, and as she was a single mother, my younger sister and I spent many a day playing by the pool with white kids from the US and UK while she finished her double shift.

At school, I quickly made friends with kids as weird as me, who invented nerdy songs and were obsessed with the Spice Girls. Though we all identified as Black, I was the only Barbadian-born member of the group. When the lunch bell rang, I noticed a large, white picnic bench under a few trees; it looked like a great place to eat my soggy tuna sandwiches.

"Not there, that's the white bench," an older student said. We were confused, until a few seconds later when a large group of white students squeezed themselves onto the bench.

They literally meant the *white* bench.

We laughed and shrugged it off. White people were the minority, so what if they felt more comfortable eating together? People gravitate towards the familiar, right?

One day we were let out of class early, and the white bench looked particularly inviting, an empty haven from the hot sun.

"Let's go sit on the white bench," I said, and we giggled at the thought of breaking the unofficial rule. The four of us ate our lunch at the bench, and when the bell rang we expected the white students to join us.

Except . . . they never came.

Soon we began to feel an angry heat that had nothing to do with the sun. The white students had gathered under a nearby tree, openly glaring at us. We squeezed closer together to show there was still enough room on the bench for everyone, but no one joined us. Their whispers floated in the wind, spooking away our appetites. Soon, we packed up our lunch and left.

We returned to our classroom in an uncomfortable silence, and then peeked over the balcony. Eventually, two white students approached the bench, and as if they telepathically indicated it was safe, everyone else followed. A few of them wiped the seat and my friends and I gave each other knowing looks.

"Maybe we left some crumbs behind," Marie said, the eternal optimist. This happens when you experience your first Glitch. It's easier to make excuses than to confront a hurtful reality. We brushed the incident aside and forgot all about it.

Years later I would relay this story to a friend, but then reassured her that the white kids in my class were nice. They never ate lunch on the white bench. They were allies. If any of them had been around that day, they would have sat next to us on that bench. Maybe their acceptance would have shown the other white kids that everyone was welcome to join us. We could have all exchanged soggy sandwiches, traded stories about teachers, and if they were up for it, belted out a few Spice Girl tunes.

Then my friend asked if I ever went to any of my white classmates' houses to hang out or was invited to their birthday parties . . . and I was silent.

BARBADOS, 2004

Growing up in a country that is majority Black is a privilege, especially for Black people. I had never been afraid to walk the streets because of the colour of my skin. Our elected politicians are Black. Our newscasters are Black. Seeing a police officer coming towards me with a grim face only brings about fears of getting a parking ticket. I've never had to think about racially motivated violence – never saw a white police officer anywhere but on TV until I visited America as a teen. Since our independence from Britain, Black people have held most visible positions of power.

But if you take a closer look, you'll see that in a country that is 92% Black, the 3% of white people control the majority of the economic wealth, thanks to the continuously reaped benefits of the transatlantic slave trade and lingering effects of colonialism.

This became clear to me during an Economics lecture at university, when the class was divided into groups to analyse annual reports for some of the most profitable conglomerates on the island. Afterwards, we came together to compare notes:

"Wait, that guy is on the board at this company, too."

"I have him, too!"

"And him as well!"

"Me, too!"

It was like we found Old White Dude bingo cards or had photocopied the board of directors with the same smiling white men for each annual report. It was an enlightening moment, like when you work out the plot twist for a movie. The 3% may not be visible on local TV or in parliament, but they are present behind the scenes, holding the invisible economic power.

It was hard to ignore that Glitch. Not when the evidence was clear on satin-coated paper. So instead, we rationalized.

"They inherited these companies from family, what were they supposed to do? Refuse the business opportunity?"

"My mother works for this man and he treats his staff like family. They're putting food on hundreds of Barbadian tables."

"Black people need to stop being so frightened and take more risks in business."

The power of the machines is strong and we needed an ally then.

I wish a student had pointed out that the white people's wealth had been accumulated over several hundred years of slavery and exploitation of the blood, sweat, death, and little-mentioned innovations of our ancestors.

That the first formerly enslaved people allowed to own land on the island did so less than two-hundred years ago, and that one had to be a property owner to have the right to vote until 1950 – approximately seventy years ago!

> **A WRITER FRIEND MENTIONED THAT HER GREAT-GREAT GRANDFATHER BOUGHT HER GREAT-GREAT GRANDMOTHER AT AN AUCTION.**

Though it was an Economics class, I wish the professor would have recognized the relevance of our history, and highlighted that when slavery was abolished, the plantation owners – the predecessors of the smiling white men on the boards – were handsomely compensated, lining their pockets even further. That less than ninety years ago, Black people on the island rose up in rebellion due to dismal labour and social conditions, still dictated by the white elites, one hundred years after the abolition of slavery.

But no one spoke up. Instead, snippets of hard truths later told the story.

Before she passed, my grandmother, who had worked on a plantation, still became tongue-tied when I brought a white friend to meet her.

A writer friend mentioned that her great-great grandfather bought her great-great grandmother at an auction.

A colleague confided that the easiest way to get a bank loan for a new small business was to get any white man as a silent partner.

CONVERSATIONS ABOUT RACE AND INEQUALITY WILL NEVER BE COMFORTABLE TO HAVE, NO MATTER THE OCCASION.

I thought about these facts when I was trying to charm a wealthy white resident to invest in a film over dinner, and they mentioned that slavery was so long ago and Black people need to get over it

I paused, the knife and fork hovering over my salmon. Sometimes when you experience a Glitch you make the excuse that the timing isn't right. Not over dinner. Not in a business setting. Not with a new acquaintance. But conversations about race and inequality will never be comfortable to have, no matter the occasion.

I wish that I was brave enough to speak out then. I wished I had witnessed more allies calling out friends and colleagues when they made ignorant statements, not with the intention to embarrass, but to educate.

I was scared. I didn't know how to tackle such a conversation. So instead, I continued to eat my meal, even though the perfectly-seasoned fish now had no taste.

EDINBURGH, SCOTLAND, 2010

For the first time, I was living in a country where I was in the minority. I went to a party with some other university students, including my classmate, Carolina, a Black woman from Portugal. She was one of the more mature students in my year, and I admired her confidence and her drive.

In a conversation at a party, I spoke about being accustomed to interacting with persons of various races and ethnicities, and that when I looked at my friends I didn't see white Greek, or white German, I saw quirky Sophia, and jovial Emily. Then I uttered the words, "I don't see colour."

Everyone nodded, but Carolina took my hand, smiling. "Shakirah, of course you see colour," she said. "If you didn't see colour, you wouldn't see me. You wouldn't see yourself."

> **IF YOU DON'T SEE COLOUR, YOU'RE ERASING OUR STRUGGLE, IGNORING OUR BATTLES.**

Though she said it in the gentlest way, shame rushed to my head. I opened my mouth to clarify I didn't mean it like that, but then realized I was making the same excuse white people made when they were called out for saying something ignorant. In that moment, instead of trying to justify my behaviour, I had to accept my own problematic views and actions. I was basically giving every white person on that balcony permission to parrot such a problematic statement.

I know some people utter these words with the best intentions, but if you don't see colour, then you don't see the discrimination forced upon millions of people. If you don't see colour, you're erasing our struggle, ignoring our battles.

That phrase never left my lips again, and now I knew how to call out someone if they made the same ignorant statement.

I think about my words every time I have to correct some well-meaning white person who claims they don't discriminate against any skin colour; black, purple, or blue, as if millions of purple people have died fighting for basic human rights, or Smurfs revolted on sugar plantations. I replay that moment at the party all the time, and get ashamed all over again. I'm grateful that Carolina was there to educate me. It's hard to call out someone in public, especially people from your own community.

Years later, I messaged Carolina and thanked her, since I had only given a stiff nod at the time. She didn't remember saying it. Small moments of speaking out can have life-changing, perspective-altering effects on others, even if they seem insignificant to you.

EDINBURGH, SCOTLAND, 2011

I was always surrounded by friends on campus, but when I enrolled in a writing course at another university, twice a week I caught the bus by myself. In those rare moments that I was alone, I stared at my reflection in the bus window and was reminded that I was a Black girl with long dreadlocks in a majority white country.

One day, I realized that the seat next to me remained vacant for a very long time. The route began near my campus and so it was often almost empty when I boarded. But by the time we reached the city centre, there was usually standing room only.

Soon I noticed that people would only sit next to me when the seat was one of the last remaining. I chided myself for being paranoid. Creating an unnecessary Glitch in the matrix.

But for fun, I created a game – Let's See When Someone Sits Next to Me. I sat near the front, and made myself as small as possible. Week after week, my seat would be one of the last to be filled. I moved positions, sitting at the front, middle, back of the bus – it changed nothing.

I kept my face turned to the window to seem as nonthreatening as possible, but it didn't help. One time, the bus almost made it all the way to the city centre, with some passengers even choosing to stand, before I felt a presence easing into the seat beside me. Soon, I started to regret these journeys to the city alone, even as I tried to find humour in my game.

One week, just when my game was about to begin, a young white woman slid into the seat beside me. I actually jumped, then tried not to move in case I scared her away. I couldn't believe it; there were still prime window seats available!

She didn't take notice of me at all – no overly polite nods, no forced half-smiles, no hesitation before sitting. She spent most of the time on her phone. I have never felt so grateful to be unnoticeable.

AN ALLY HAS TO DO CONSTANT SELF-INTERROGATION BECAUSE IT'S HARD TO CORRECT A BIAS THAT YOU DON'T KNOW EXISTS.

When she got off the bus, I wanted to wave goodbye. She'd never know how much her short companionship meant to me.

How could she? Until then, when I was struggling to hold back tears while she sat there, I had no idea how much it hurt to play the game.

I don't believe every single person who didn't sit next to me was racist. Some of them may have considered themselves to be allies to marginalized communities, but an ally has to do constant self-interrogation because it's hard to correct a bias that you don't know exists.

I don't expect anyone else would be playing Let's See When Someone Sits Next to Me. But whenever I board a bus overseas, I take a seat next to a person of colour, especially if their face is turned towards the window, just in case.

PHILADELPHIA, UNITED STATES, 2012

One of my aunts – who had never stepped foot off the island – would frown while watching US news reports and tut, "why are African Americans so angry?" She'd complain about the gangsters and drug addicts creating bad neighbourhoods, and giving Black people a bad reputation. Unfortunately, many Caribbean people, who thought themselves superior to the "violent" African Americans portrayed on TV, shared her sentiments. Sometimes Black people can be unknowing Agents of the system.

I was excited about this trip to Philadelphia to visit my friend Marie from the Bahamas, who was now a student at university.

Marie and I were walking downtown when at least ten police cars sped past, lights and sirens blaring. They screeched and made U-turns on the other side of the road, and officers jumped out, guns armed and ready. I felt like a bystander in one of those cop shows on TV. Then, four of the police officers grabbed two young Black men and shoved them onto the ground.

Marie and I stopped, and stepped under a shop awning to avoid the other pedestrians, who didn't break stride.

It seemed so unnecessary to have all these police officers here, just to arrest two men, so I was convinced there was a bigger catastrophe at hand. It probably wasn't the wisest decision to stay; if there was a bomb we would have been wiped away, but we were rooted to the spot.

Suddenly, the demeanour of all the officers changed. They put away their guns, leant against cars, and laughed. If I were a cartoon character my mouth would have fallen onto the floor. Marie and I looked on in confusion as the police officers removed the handcuffs on the two men, and then drove off.

We went to see if the men were okay and found out what happened. The police officers were looking for thieves who had robbed a nearby shop. They thought that the young Black men fit the description of the suspects, but then got a call that the actual perpetrators were apprehended.

The boys shrugged.

Shrugged! Like if the police had asked them for directions instead of planting their bodies into the ground like seeds.

"Why aren't you more upset?" I asked, looking at them in disbelief.

"This happens all the time."

They thanked us for staying, and then walked away. We stood there, gaping at their backs, until they disappeared into the flood of pedestrians, who still had not paused. I thought about my aunt shaking her head, and frowning at the television, and knew I needed to face reality.

I had been in America for two days, and I was angry, too.

NEW YORK, UNITED STATES, 2012

A few days after the incident in Philadelphia, I packed my suitcase and headed to the Big Apple. You know those movies where the country girl moves to the city, and we see her head sticking out of a cab, gaping up at skyscrapers that kissed clouds? That was me. I had a blast exploring Times Square and Broadway.

But then reality kicked in – the noise and chaos, and my expressions of wonder were replaced by fear when I had to unravel the subway and train system, attempting to make my way to a friend in the neighbouring state of New Jersey.

Thankfully, I found my way to the correct station in suburban New Jersey. The worst part of the journey was over. According to her directions, all I had to do now was get a taxi from the station to her apartment, seven minutes away.

Turns out it was easier for me to navigate the subway than it was to get a taxi.

There was a line of cabs with drivers, but when I went to give the first one the address, he said he wasn't working.

Neither was the cab behind him.

Or the next.

I held on to the I ♥ NY hat I had just bought in Times Square, looked up at the darkening sky, and tried not to panic. But this wasn't New York. There were no taxis zipping up and down every half-second. There was only this bunch of defunct taxis – a cab graveyard with drivers paying respects in the front seats.

I kept walking down the line. No. No. No. Some didn't speak; they just dismissed me with a wave of their hand. Some avoided my question and stared down at newspapers.

Finally, when I was about to give up, a driver waved me over.

Cautiously, I leaned over when I got close. "Hello, are you working?"

"Yes, hop in. I'll take you," he responded.

I was relieved. I relaxed in the back seat, finally able to admire the quiet neighbourhood now that I was safe.

"Ignore them," the driver said, breaking the silence. "They're idiots."

"Who?" I replied, confused.

"The other drivers."

"Oh no, they weren't working," I said, correcting him.

"Oh, they were working!" he exclaimed.

Now I was more confused. "So why didn't they want to take me?"

I remember the driver looking into the rear-view mirror. He adjusted it; as though he wanted to see me clearly, make sure that he wasn't making a mistake.

"Because you're Black!" he yelled. My eyes widened in shock, and a little embarrassment to be honest. It was only then I realized that he was Black, too, and the other taxi drivers had

been of other races. I might as well have been wearing
Barbados's national costume because it was clear I was an
outsider and didn't understand the dynamics of this matrix. But I
had enough. That Black taxi driver didn't know it, but he pushed
me down the rabbit hole, and I had a clear view of harsh reality.

After the shock wore off, I became angry. Again. It was 2012.
Barack Obama – the first Black president of the United States –
had just been elected for a second term. People were
celebrating the accomplishment as evidence that racism
no longer existed in the country.

Yet, if it weren't for a taximan, who didn't see me as a Bajan,
Caribbean, African, or African American, but as a fellow Black
person in need of assistance, I would have been stranded at an
empty station in New Jersey.

BARBADOS, 2020

With the rise of the Black Lives Matter movement in the US,
it became harder for the world to maintain the matrix. That
movement has spread across the globe, impacting even the
shores of Barbados, finally disrupting the mirage and exposing
wounds that never had the space to heal.

When Barbadians witnessed protesters in the US topple statues
of American slaveowners and Confederate monuments, eyes
inevitably turned to the bronze statue of British Admiral Lord
Nelson, a keen supporter of the transatlantic slave trade and
the British empire, that had been towering in the middle of the
city centre in our renamed National Heroes Square since 1813.
There had been a resolution in the 1990s to have this statue

removed, followed by decades of sporadic debate, but it was only after a local Black Lives Matter protest and a #NelsonMustGo petition, that the government made an incredible announcement: Nelson was coming down.

Suddenly, the statue, which is located in an area not often frequented by upper classes of society, became an important symbol of white Barbadian history. Several white Bajans took to social media to denounce the relocation of the statue to the museum since it would be "erasing our history". One white business owner insisted that she was tired of hearing about racism and seeing hate towards white people, especially in the height of tourist season. She insisted that "Blacks get rid of the chip on their shoulder to move forward."

Another comment that received support from their community came from a white man who claimed that Barbados's independence from Britain was the most racist act, one that lowered the standard of living on the island, and moving the Nelson statue was another racist action that would come at a high cost.

Suddenly the mirage of racial harmony was broken. The matrix was temporarily shut down and #ScreenshotARacist became a local social media campaign.

Expletives were shared. Families divided. Friendships broken. Businesses cancelled. Employees fired. Racists went back into hiding. People went back to living.

But one thing was clear: it took more than thirty years to remove the statue, a symbol of our colonial past, but it will take much longer to remove the lingering stench of racism and segregation on the island. We can no longer pretend it does not exist.

There's so much more I want to talk about – why I sometimes feel sad when I visit museums since I'm reminded that my own history

> **I AM UNCOMFORTABLE WITH PLANTATIONS WHO GIVE GUIDED TOURS WITHOUT MENTIONING THEIR COLONIAL AND SLAVE-OWNING PAST, AND CROC-WEARING TOURISTS TRAMPLE ON THE UNMARKED GRAVES OF THE ENSLAVED TO SAMPLE RUM.**

has been destroyed. Why I got offended when a white man shared a photo from 1900s Barbados and lamented about the "good ole days", a time when my ancestors were disenfranchised of basic human rights. Why I am uncomfortable with plantations who give guided tours without mentioning their colonial and slave-owning past, and Croc-wearing tourists trample on the unmarked graves of the enslaved to sample rum. But there is no word count large enough to cover all the overt and subtle prejudices faced by Black people every single day.

I needed allies who could disrupt the system so many times, even when I didn't know it. A white student could have joined us on that white bench. Someone could have given pseudo-intellectual Economics students a history lesson and called us out on our ignorant statements, just like Carolina did at the party. More strangers could have sat next to me on the bus . . .

Allyship is a never-ending journey. I have to actively work towards recognizing signs of subtle racism, and the mechanics of systemic racism that continues to manifest itself in multiple forms to disenfranchise marginalized people around the world. I still make mistakes and have to be educated. But choosing to be an ally is to continuously listen, learn, improve, question, and then reeducate others, and always, always paying attention to the Glitches.

STUTTER BUDDY

DERICK BROOKS

Sometimes talking is like travelling through a maze.

Most of us can get through it pretty easily.

Some even easier.

I didn't realize it's not always that simple until I met *Lauren*.

She's the cleverest, coolest, funniest person I know.

But also, she stutters.

When it happens it's like she's blocked by a wall that only exists for her.

She can't jump over it.

She can't go around it.

Sometimes she can find a different path.

Sometimes she can press into it.

Either way she might run into it again.

It makes some people uncomfortable, but that's on them.

I think she's cool.

Choosing to tell people about her stutter can be exhausting.

She doesn't do it to make them feel better.

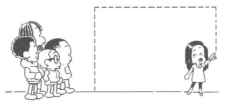

She does it to take care of herself, because her thoughts and feelings are important.

And I promise you . . .

It's worth the wait.

THIS IS WHAT IT FEELS LIKE

A.J. SASS

AUTUMN

. . . feels like summer everywhere else, because weather in the Bay Area, California, is just as quirky as the residents who call it home.

What it doesn't feel like? Pride season.

But because of the overwhelming popularity of San Francisco's Pride event in June – where a million visitors flood the streets over a single, celebratory weekend – September is when neighbouring Oakland holds its festivities.

That's where I find myself one sun-kissed autumn afternoon. My friends and I have chosen to picnic at a park close to the official Oakland Pride parade route. Owen (he/him) sits by my side, his bleached blond hair shaved short.

There are others in our group, virtually every shade of queer identity present and accounted for. Most are folks I met at a group therapy session for trans and questioning young adults a few months earlier.

We talk about our jobs (overworked, underpaid), the weather (finally warm after a frigid, foggy summer), the upcoming presidential election (Obama versus Romney). All the while,

I wait for a lull in the conversation, for my chance to share a vital piece in what feels like the increasingly complex puzzle of my life.

I've psyched myself out before, back in June during the San Francisco Trans March. That's when Owen revealed his new name. I didn't want to dilute his news with my own announcement.

But in the months since the Trans March, the thought of sharing my own new name has grown into something bigger, scarier.

I take a breath as Dom (she/her) peels back the lid of a salsa container and her boyfriend, Oak (he/him), tosses Owen a bag of tortilla chips.

One long exhalation, then a rush of words. "I think I've figured out my name."

Their focus shifts. All eyes on me. My chest flutters, like a butterfly trapped in a mason jar.

Sharing a new name feels permanent, irreversible, but also necessary. Among friends, I am A (who-the-heck-knows-yet on pronouns), the first initial of my birth name. I haven't gotten that far with my coworkers, resigning myself to prickling discomfort every time they unknowingly misgender me.

I could shrug this off with a laugh and a quick shake of my head. Never mind. Just kidding.

Except, I don't want to take a step back. It's exhausting to juggle multiple identities.

"I'm going with Andrew." I swallow hard. "I think?"

Not the confident declaration I envisioned, but at least it's out.

"Cool." Owen leans forward, dipping a chip into our communal salsa. "You know you can always change it later, too, if you end up not liking it."

> **THE BUTTERFLY IN MY CHEST FLIES UP, THEN OUT THROUGH MY RIBS. THE JAR WAS A TEMPORARY PRISON. IT NEVER HAD A LID TO BEGIN WITH.**

A contingent of parade participants snakes towards us on the street below our hill. Music starts up. Heavy bass thrums in my throat.

"Yeah?"

"Totally. I must've tried half a dozen names before I landed on Owen."

It seems so obvious now that he's said it, but still. You don't know what you don't know.

"I was Pine for, like, two weeks a few years ago," Oak offers. "But it always made me think of the cleaning solution."

Owen laughs, then nudges me. "Andrew for now, though?"

The butterfly in my chest flies up, then out through my ribs. The jar was a temporary prison. It never had a lid to begin with.

I nod as hundreds of rainbow flags flutter below us. "Andrew for now."

Autumn feels like a fresh start, so full of potential.

WINTER

. . . feels like time to write a novel.

For years, that's exactly what I do. Every November, I commit to writing a minimum of 1,667 words per day to hit the fabled 50K that makes you a winner of National Novel Writing Month (NaNoWriMo).

If you live in the Bay Area (or are willing to travel here), you can even attend the noir-themed Night of Writing Dangerously, NaNoWriMo's annual fundraiser.

The Julia Morgan Ballroom is a lavish venue in San Francisco's Financial District: tall ceilings, thick velvet curtains, golden crown moulding. I'd attended last year, but that was different. It was pre-transition, when I had another job, accompanied by a former partner.

This is the first time I'm here on my own, decked out in braces, a small-brim fedora, and Oxford shirt. Authentically Andrew – or at least a little closer.

I choose a seat at one of a dozen round tables. A stack of name tags forms the centrepiece. I fill one out, then press it onto my chest, just over my heart. Right now, most people are mingling with old friends or browsing a buffet table filled with every type of candy imaginable. Others are at the bar, ordering drinks with clever writing pun names.

I set up my laptop, preparing for a night of writing sprints on my fragmentary draft of a YA sci-fi story.

"Are these seats free?"

Another Wrimo writer looks down at me, wearing a similar outfit to mine (minus braces). A tie holds back sleek, black hair in a loose ponytail.

I nod. Watch them lean towards the centre of the table, then fill out a name tag: Grace.

Grace waves at someone by the bar. Two someones, actually. Each drops a laptop bag at their feet, then fills out a name tag.

Tall, dark-haired Mark takes a seat beside Grace, across the table from me. I receive a small nod, then both settle in.

A glimpse of the other Wrimo makes my stomach twist. I don't have to look at her name tag to remember short, curly-haired Tammy. We shared a table last year, back before I was Andrew, or even A.

She knows me by my birth name.

Maybe it's the dim lighting, or my shorter hair, but Tammy doesn't say anything that implies she recognizes me. We say a round of hellos, then everyone unpacks their laptops and notebooks. I allow myself to relax a little.

It doesn't last long.

Because Mark keeps glancing at me from under the rim of his fedora. By now, the scrutiny feels familiar. I get looks like this often enough, even in progressive, come-as-you-are San Francisco.

I hunch over my laptop and adjust my hat so it covers more of my face, wishing people didn't have the inherent need to categorize every little thing.

Right | Wrong

Taken | Single

Boy | Girl

In some ways, I get it. I know categories help avoid confusion. I also know that a traditionally boy's name stuck to my chest

doesn't address all the other aspects of my appearance that imply the opposite.

I wait for the question I know is coming. My braces weigh down on my tense shoulders.

"Hey," Mark says. "Pass me that marker."

By the time I look up, Grace has already handed it over. Mark strips off his name tag in one smooth motion, scribbles something, then puts it back on.

I blink at his tag:

Mark

He, him, his

Mark catches me looking. "I'm usually way more on top of these things."

My tension drains away as Grace adds *she/her* to her name tag, then passes the marker to Tammy. The *she + her* isn't a surprise to me here, but it's still nice to know for sure.

The marker reaches me. I write a careful *he*, trying it on for size. Since quitting my job earlier this month, I haven't been thinking about pronouns as much, but I know I'll eventually have to figure them out.

This time when Mark looks at me, he smiles instead of furrowing his brows.

A Night of Writing Dangerously organizer steps up to a podium, then announces the first official writing sprint of the night. Our focus shifts to our notebooks and laptops, heads bowed, fingers a rapid blur. Every second matters. Each word counts.

Throughout the evening, we chat about our novels, what part of the city we live in, what we do with our lives when we're not trying to write a manuscript in such a short span of time. Dinner comes and goes. We get up and stretch, have author portraits taken by a professional photographer, and listen to inspirational speeches from fellow Wrimos.

As midnight approaches, we grab milk and cookies before the final sprint. I trade numbers with all three of them, setting up a time to meet Mark later in the week to write together.

When the event ends, I say goodbye to Mark and Grace who head off in one direction. Tammy and I walk the other way together.

"Want to share a taxi?" I ask her.

She shakes her head. "I'm walking distance. But I'll wait with you."

It's not long before my taxi rolls up. I wave to Tammy, then pull open the door.

"Hey, Andrew," she says.

I turn back to her.

"Your new name suits you well."

Winter feels like a friendly nod. Like validation.

SPRING

. . . feels like a last-ditch attempt to fulfil winter resolutions.

That's why I accept when Mark invites me to work out at his gym one day in early April – even though the thought forms a thick knot in my stomach.

It's not that I haven't wanted to work out since I joined a gym in January. It's that bodies tell stories; mine wasn't telling the right one to a patron in the men's locker room at my last gym.

Are you trying to make a political statement or something?

His voice still echoes in my mind, although I wasn't even stripping down like everyone else. I'd worn shorts under my street clothes, not that it mattered.

His tone was clear: You don't belong.

Mark's gym is on the same street as mine. Located in San Francisco's famously gay Castro neighbourhood, this stretch of Market Street is dotted with them. I'm not convinced trading one gym for another will be an improvement, but Mark and I have gotten close over the past few months, when I was between full-time jobs. While he sipped black coffee and worked on his novel at various cafes, I hunkered down with a sugary latte, writing freelance blog posts. Grace sometimes joined us.

Now I've got a new job, where I finally get to be myself. Correct name, male pronouns, thanks to a supportive boss. I can't make our weekday writing meetups anymore, so working out is one of the only times Mark and I can spend together.

Except that question-that-wasn't-really-a-question still gnaws at me.

As we take the stairs up to Mark's gym, my mind floods with belated comebacks.

My favourite:

I leave the politics for my ballot, thanks. Right now, I'm just trying to change.

Admittedly not great, but it's much better than what actually happened. I'd frozen, managing a barely audible "no," before escaping to the nearest toilet cubicle.

Mark doesn't know this. I've kept it to myself like a shameful secret.

Now, I can't help giving him an out.

"Should I use the women's locker room here?"

Mark pauses in front of the entrance. "Do you want to use the women's locker room?"

I shake my head as he holds the door open for me.

> **BODIES TELL STORIES, WHETHER WE WANT THEM TO OR NOT. I CAN'T HELP WONDERING WHAT STORY MINE WILL TELL IF I START TAKING TESTOSTERONE.**

"So you'll use the men's," he says, like that settles it.

He signs me in as his guest, then we make our way into the locker room.

Inside, we pass a line of showers, separated by tile walls. This room is much smaller than the one at my gym. It's just an open space with a row of lockers. Nowhere to go if someone doesn't want me in here.

We're alone, for now. Not taking a second for granted, I change clothes as fast as I can. My workout shorts are already beneath my jeans, a sports bra and baggy T-shirt under my hoodie.

Out in the gym, Mark and I warm up on treadmills. Then he walks me through proper free-weight lifting technique.

I study Mark's every movement, memorizing not just the technique but also his body's contours. Wide at his shoulders, Mark's waist tapers like an upside-down triangle. I'm the opposite, with a slender upper body that goes wide at my hips.

Bodies tell stories, whether we want them to or not. I can't help wondering what story mine will tell if I start taking testosterone. Owen started months ago and already seems happy with his results. I'm still on the fence.

This time we're not alone when we return to the locker room.

"Want to grab some dinner?" Mark asks.

"Sure."

He peels off his sweaty shirt, either unaware of the two guys changing nearby or else unconcerned.

And why would he be? His body tells a straightforward story. Mine's full of plot twists.

He grabs a pair of towels and passes me one. "All good?"

Throat dry, I take the towel with a quick nod.

He heads off towards the showers. I turn away from the other two guys but can't make myself strip down like Mark did. Instead, I tuck my clean clothes under one arm and practically sprint to the nearest empty shower cubicle.

Only once I've confirmed the curtain is completely closed do I slip out of my clothes. I hang everything up on the metal curtain rod, then clean up.

By the time I'm done, Mark's already back in the locker area, voice drifting to me as he chats with another gym patron. I slide into my underwear and jeans, then look down at myself. Bare-chested, I don't look like any guy I've ever seen.

But maybe I'm reading this book all wrong. Maybe my chest isn't telling the story of a girl. What if it's just saying "Andrew?"

I drape the towel over my shoulders, then step out of the shower before I can second-guess myself. The towel's terrycloth ends mostly cover my chest.

This is a test, I decide. An experiment. I make my way back to the lockers.

Immediate regret. Now there are three guys.

"Hey, Andrew," Mark says as I drop my sweaty clothes on a bench. "This is Chris."

We exchange quick greetings, then Chris claims a locker across the room. It's only when I've shoved all my used clothes into my duffel bag that I realize I've made a fatal error in my calculations: I'm going to have to drop the towel to put on my shirt – unless I want to put it on over a wet towel, which, gross.

Mark takes a seat, then pulls out his phone. "I'm going to check if Grace wants to grab food with us."

A quick glance around shows no one's looking at me. I take my chance, letting the towel slide off my shoulders. In the same motion, I reach for my shirt, fumbling with the collar as I try to figure out which side is the front. My pulse pounds in my ears.

"How do you feel about sushi?"

I startle and the shirt drops to the bench. Cheeks burning, I can't bring myself to look over at Mark, or even cover myself up. This feels just like my last gym trip, except instead of politics, my downfall today is raw fish.

My shirt rises into view. I glance over at it, then down the length of Mark's arm. Our eyes meet. He's looking at me like normal. We could be in line at a store, waiting for the light to turn at a crossing. Anywhere.

"Sushi's fine." I try to put my shirt on at a normal speed but I'm probably still rushing. Chris gives me a quick smile as he heads out of the locker room. The other two aren't looking my way at all. I'm just one of the guys to them, getting changed after a workout.

All because Mark's treating me like one.

My pulse gradually slows.

Mark stands, swinging his duffel over one shoulder. "Grace said she can meet us in ten."

This time, I hold the door open for him when we exit the gym.

SPRING FEELS LIKE PERMISSION TO BE MYSELF, NO MATTER WHAT STORY OTHERS THINK MY BODY TELLS.

He looks over at me as we take the stairs down to Market Street. "So, what did you think?"

I take a breath of the air, still crisp with a final hint of winter. "I think I'm going to be switching gyms."

Spring feels like permission to be myself, no matter what story others think my body tells.

SUMMER

. . . feels like one long party, starting with Pride Month in June.

June is also when I take my first dose of testosterone, under the supervision of my doctor. A month later, my friends throw me a "T-party" in San Francisco's Dolores Park to celebrate the milestone. Mark is out of town, but Grace comes, as do Owen, Oak, and a handful of other people I've met at various events.

It's unusually warm for a July in the city and the afternoon feels festive. We're not the only ones picnicking on this gorgeous, sun-drenched day, but we've carved out a little space for ourselves, under the shade of a tree.

> THE TRANS GUY LABEL FEELS LIKE IT FITS ME ABOUT AS WELL AS A T-SHIRT THAT'S THREE SIZES TOO SMALL.

"So, explain why this guy you're dating thought he needed to call 911 after your T shot?" Owen pops one of Grace's homemade kale chips into his mouth. "I feel like I only got half of the story from your texts."

"It wasn't his fault." I try to hide my smile.

"I just didn't know some syringes have needles that auto-retract. The ones my doctor used definitely didn't."

Owen and Oak both nod. Apparently I'm the only one who didn't get the memo.

"So, it was my first time injecting at home and everything was going fine. But then the needle just disappeared after I pushed the plunger completely down." I shake my head, mildly embarrassed. "He wasn't the only one freaking out. I seriously thought I'd broken the needle off in my leg."

Laughter erupts from my friends.

"What a first date," Oak crows.

"Technically," I deadpan, "it was our third."

Owen nudges me. "Trans guy problems, right?"

A twinge of discomfort. Even though we're going through many of the same steps to medically transition, the trans guy label feels like it fits me about as well as a T-shirt that's three sizes too small.

"Something like that."

"So." Owen refills his paper cup with iced tea. "Have you noticed any changes yet?"

I side-eye him. "After a month?"

"Hey, you could be an early bloomer!"

"I'm not." Another twinge. "And honestly? I don't even know if I feel like a man yet."

"Give it time. It'll happen," Oak says. He's been on T the longest of all of us. "Especially when people stop misgendering you."

I reach for Grace's kale chips.

"I didn't believe it either," Owen tells me, "but it's definitely a thing. Just a few more months and you'll see."

He takes off his shirt and lays back, using it as a headrest. Faint scars smile up at me from under both of his pecs, the result of his top surgery a few months back. They've healed nicely, now barely noticeable. I wonder how my chest will look after my own surgery, scheduled for this autumn.

I nod but don't respond. Time might change a lot of things, but I've been waiting all year for my feelings to shift on a similar trajectory with my body. They haven't. "Woman" isn't the right word for me, but "man" doesn't fit perfectly either.

And lately, I've been getting so frustrated with how binary the world feels.

Toilets and locker rooms.

Clothes.

Even computers speak in ones and zeros.

Oak waves a Frisbee and Owen gets up to join him for a game. Grace scoots closer to me. I sit with her in comfortable silence as thoughts swirl in my mind.

"Everything okay?"

"Sure." I shrug. "Why wouldn't it be?"

She takes a sip from her paper cup. "Just checking. You went quiet."

I sigh. Chew on a kale chip.

"I seriously don't think I'll ever feel like a man," I finally tell her, "even if I'm on T for years."

"Okay." She sits with this for a beat. "Well, maybe you aren't one. Just because Owen and Oak had similar experiences doesn't mean yours isn't valid because it's been different."

I don't know what she means, but her words immediately calm me.

"Now." Grace lays her head on my shoulder. "Tell me about this guy you've been seeing . . ."

Summer suddenly feels full of possibilities.

A YEAR

. . . feels like progress, but not as much as I thought it would.

It's easy to look back now, years later, armed with the knowledge that transition looks different for every trans person. There is no one right way to discover who you are.

When I first came out as a transgender, I hadn't heard the term "non-binary" yet. Plus, all the trans narratives I could find online talked about knowing who you are from a young age. Even my own friends said they knew when they were kids.

That wasn't my experience.

A year after Oakland Pride, the Night of Writing Dangerously, my renewed commitment to workouts, and the Dolores Park T-party, I will hear the term non-binary for the first time. I'll let its definition build in my mind – not relating to, composed of, or involving just two things – until I can see the shape of it. Until I recognize it for what it's always been.

An image of myself, reflecting back at me.

Two years later, I will leave my beloved San Francisco for a small town where no one knows my background. I'll settle into the labels others give me because being seen as a gay man seems

> **FOR THE FIRST TIME, A LABEL WILL FEEL LIKE IT FITS PROPERLY; RATHER THAN SETTLING FOR TERMS OTHERS GIVE ME, THIS WORD WILL BECOME A POINT OF PRIDE THAT I'LL CLAIM AS MINE . . .**

less complicated for people to grasp than being trans. My friends and I will try to keep in touch, although some of us will grow apart.

Five years from now, I'll write a book about a non-binary ice skater. It'll feel liberating to explore the gendered components of a sport I've trained in since I was a kid. Grace will read it, provide feedback. I'll query literary agents and sign with one I'm excited to work with.

As my agent prepares my manuscript for submission to publishers, she'll ask if I'm comfortable with her pitching me as a non-binary author. She'll tell me she supports me no matter my decision.

Six years, and that book will sell. I'll share the news on social media and come out to my friends and family for a second time.

I will make the decision to discontinue testosterone and update my pronouns. Expand them, actually, making room alongside he, his, him for they, their, them. I'll feel a small thrill whenever people use them interchangeably to refer to me.

The guy I met six summers ago, now my boyfriend, will embrace these changes. Same for my friends. They'll offer to throw me another party, although distance precludes it becoming reality.

Eight years, and I'll become a debut author, penning essays about my journey to discovering I'm non-binary. For the first time, a label will feel like it fits properly; rather than settling for terms others give me, this word will become a point of pride that I'll claim as mine, wholeheartedly. During my virtual book launch event, I'll get asked a question by an eleven-year-old non-binary kid about what it's like to live in the world as a non-binary adult. This is the moment I'll finally know that my struggles to define myself on my own terms have been worth it.

A year might not feel like a long time, but years add up.

Every single one has brought me closer to the person I am now.

6

"WHY DIDN'T ANYONE ELSE SAY ANYTHING?"

NAOMI AND NATALIE EVANS

"We have to repent in this generation not merely for the hateful words and actions of the bad people but for the appalling silence of the good people." – Dr Martin Luther King, Jr, "Letter from Birmingham Jail", 1963

NATALIE

It was late October and I was at the train station in London travelling back to my small hometown by the sea. It was a sunny Friday afternoon, but the air was cold enough to see the condensation from my mouth when I breathed out.

I had just finished a full day of work that involved a lot of meetings, coffee, and dull conversation, so I was very tired and ready for the weekend ahead. I stood on the platform in my thick coat and a scarf, wishing I had driven that day. The clock turned 3:25, and two bright circle lights entered through the tunnel.

"Finally," I thought. I waited for passengers to get off before I stepped on the train and found two single seats available. Then I put in my headphones, tilted my head on the glass window next to me, and closed my eyes while the train sped off to the next stop.

As my podcast played I heard a faint announcement in the background as the train slowed down at the next stop. When I opened my eyes, I saw two white men, both wearing black coats, jeans, and carrying a supermarket bag which I imagine had the remaining cans of beer that they were holding in their hands. They were speaking like they were in a nightclub, where you have to shout over the music to hold a conversation. Other passengers noticeably shuffled their bodies and moved to attention. Ears pricked up – some people looked up and away quickly while others rolled their eyes to show their disapproval at the lack of train etiquette.

All I wanted was a quiet journey home. I hoped they wouldn't be on the train for much longer.

As I scanned the carriage once again, I noticed something that wasn't very unusual to me; everyone else was white. I am mixed-race. My dad is Black Jamaican and my mum is white British, so I have brown skin along with big curly afro hair. I grew up in a very white area in Kent where most of my life I was the only person – apart from my two sisters – that looked like me in the room.

The two men were two seats away from me. I could see them between the gap in the seats and the reflection of a man in a black jacket, still clutching his beer, in the train window. Once they sat down, I closed my eyes again, leaned back on the glass window, and tried to nap once more.

The nap didn't last very long. I was interrupted by the booming voice of the conductor asking for tickets. I took my headphones out and pulled out my train ticket, ready for when he approached. The train conductor was a Black man. It's not unusual for me to notice people's race; even though my town has become more diverse and multicultural, I am still surprised when I see a Black person in the area.

I smiled and passed over my train ticket, he gave me a nod and I nodded back. This is very normal in the Black community – it's like an acknowledgement, a code for "I see you, I understand, I get what it's like to be Black in this world." I watched him walk down the carriage, asking the other passengers for their tickets, and I looked at the two loud drunk men. In my gut I knew not to put my headphones back in.

You see, when you're used to being the minority in the room you tend to pick up on certain things when in public spaces. You know when situations feel unsafe or when people are hostile towards you. You sense when to not trust a person; it's an instinct and it's one that I've gotten very used to over the years.

The train conductor walked over to the two drunk men and said, "Tickets please." There was silence, so he repeated, "Tickets please," again silence. I stared at the man with the supermarket bag in between the train seats, snickering to his friend. The conductor repeated himself again, but this time his tone was agitated and short.

Finally, the man with the supermarket bag responded without looking up, "We are getting off at the next stop, mate."

The train conductor replied, "That's not how it works, it doesn't matter if you get off at the next stop, you still need the ticket before getting on the train."

This went back and forth for about 30 seconds. The conversation between them was getting much louder and at this point more people started to pay attention. My instincts were right. After the train conductor explained that they would need a ticket in order to continue the journey the man with the supermarket bag replied, "Did you get a f***ing passport to get into the country?"

It was at that point my ears pricked up like a cat when they hear it's time for a bath. I scrambled around in my pocket, got out my phone, and pressed record.

This was my second step of being an ally.

You see, step one was realizing that this was not a safe space for the conductor. Being an ally means anticipating when someone may need support. It's about understanding the power dynamics within a room.

The train conductor's face dropped; he had a combination of facial expressions – shocked, angry, and embarrassed. I could see in his face he didn't know what to do. The next five minutes were a blur; without the phone recording I don't think I would've been able to remember what happened next. As soon as I pressed record, the train conductor sat down next to the two drunk men.

I was very surprised when he decided to sit next to them. I wondered if it was to try and deescalate the situation, maybe coming down to their level meant that they could have a conversation, rather than standing over them intensifying an argument. He then asked in an upset and slightly angry voice, "What has me having a passport got to do with your train ticket?"

It was unclear what one of the men was trying to explain but it didn't matter by this point. What he had said was racist and he was not willing to apologize for it.

The train conductor's voice got louder and his hands became more expressive. He kept repeating, "What has me having a passport got to do with your train ticket?" He told the man that his comment was racist.

> **BEING AN ALLY MEANS ANTICIPATING WHEN SOMEONE MAY NEED SUPPORT. IT'S ABOUT UNDERSTANDING THE POWER DYNAMICS WITHIN A ROOM.**

The white man responded, "I've got two mixed-race children and this guy thinks I'm racist." The train conductor shook his head, gave a loud sigh, and stood up to walk away. He was finished; the man was not listening and now had brought out his get-out-of-jail-free card, his mixed-race children.

I can relate to this feeling in so many ways. Someone has said something offensive, you challenge it, but it's game over. Defensiveness kicks in. White fragility comes into play and there is nowhere to go but to walk away. Yet, the man with the supermarket bag was still not finished. "It's always the Black card with you innit."

My blood was boiling. I was raging and everything inside me wanted to explode. There were so many things about this situation that were problematic but to then bring in mixed-race children and the race card? I could not just sit there and record this incident anymore, I had to say something. Before I knew it I stood up and without a thought, I opened my mouth.

This was step three of my allyship that day. I didn't have a well-planned-out speech, but the fact that no one else spoke up meant whatever I said was better than silence.

"Are you listening to what you have just said, it's RACIST," I said in a loud voice. He sat there and looked at me with both hands on the table, one hand still clenched around his can of beer.

"Are you serious?" he replied.

> **I COULD NOT JUST SIT THERE AND RECORD THIS INCIDENT ANYMORE, I HAD TO SAY SOMETHING.**

I continued. "Just because you have mixed-race children does not give you the right to say what you just said. Why are you asking him if he had a passport? Would you have said that if he was white?"

The guy seemed to have an answer for everything: "But," "I," "Whatever," "I am not racist."

"What has your train ticket got to do with his passport?"

He looked away from me and hung his head, like a puppy who couldn't look at his owner after chewing up the sofa. He tried one more time, "Oh my god I can't say anything anymore . . . "

"Don't start playing the victim now. Explain why you said it."

He sat back and sighed. He had nothing, no answer that would get him out of this mess.

I think he was shocked that I challenged him. He got up and went to apologize to the train conductor. His friend stayed in his seat. He had not said one word throughout the whole incident. The man looked defeated; I think he knew he had messed up but it was too late, the damage was already done.

I sat down and I turned off the recording. I was shaking, my voice was shaking, my hands were shaking, my body was shaking, and I was utterly devastated.

These incidents were nothing new to me. I am used to them; however, the one thing that upset me the most, even more than having to challenge racist comments, was that not one other person intervened.

Not. One.

The woman sitting in front of me put a scarf around her head as if it would make her invisible. The man opposite me moved his newspaper closer to his face so that he could pretend he couldn't see what was happening. Two younger guys beside me looked shocked, like rabbits in the headlights, not knowing what to do or say.

When I looked around the carriage, people who were staring at me dodged my gaze. One woman looked at me in disgust and shook her head; clearly, I had ruined her journey home.

I decided to move carriages as I didn't want to be near any of them anymore. I sat down, still shaking, slammed my bag on the chair, and let out a big sigh. As the train slowed down to a stop, I looked out the window and saw the two men in their black jackets, still holding their cans of beer while walking away.

A few minutes later, the train conductor came over and thanked me, to which I responded, "There is nothing to thank me for. I am so sorry this happened to you." I explained I had it on video and if he needed, I could send it to him to report to the police. We then both carried on with the train ride, and it felt like the longest journey in the world.

When the train stopped at the next station and people got up to leave the carriage, a few people from the previous carriage walked over to me and said well done. I felt so angry. I wanted to respond with, "Where were you?", "Why didn't you say anything?", "This shouldn't be my fight."

Why were the only Black and Brown people (me and the train conductor) the ones to say something? Why didn't white people use their privilege in that moment?

As soon as I got off the train, I called my sister, Naomi. The person I knew would understand.

I told her the story and explained how embarrassed I was and that I thought I handled the situation terribly. I thought about all the things I could have said but it was too late.

However, Naomi asked the same question that I have asked many times growing up, when I left meetings at work, on nights out with friends, family gatherings, and even church socials. "Why did nobody else say anything?"

NAOMI

I was walking home from my local shop when I answered the phone call from Natalie. I was expecting her to tell me what time she would be home, but instead I was met with a shaky voice and crying. Natalie is six years younger than me and I've always been a protective big sister. I stopped in my tracks and was instantly alert.

"What's wrong?" I quickly asked.

"Na, something horrible just happened on the train," she sobbed.

As I listened, I knew exactly what she was going to say. It wasn't unusual for me to hear about racist incidents. From ignorant phrases to outright violence, I have faced racism my whole life. It was something that I lamentably accepted as part of everyday life. It was something we as a family were used to and although it was still deeply upsetting, it was not surprising.

Every time a new incident happened it was another reminder of older ones, like opening up an old wound. The ignorant things people said to you at school that reminded you that you were the Brown girl. "You're coloured/half-caste." "Can I touch your hair? It looks like candy floss." "You're really well spoken." "Where are you really from?"

All of these incidents served to give the same reminder: you were not like them. You were "other" and as much as you tried to brush it off, your experiences would never be understood. I spent most of my teenage years trying to fit in but also knowing deep down that I wasn't really being myself.

My relationship with my hair was one of the most damaged. Constant straightening, chemicals, hair dye, and weaves, all in an attempt to look like the women I saw around me and in the magazines.

When I was growing up, hair, beauty, and fashion were centred around Eurocentric ideals, and there was scarcely any other representation and no Black hairdressers or salons. I would optimistically go to the white hairdressers clutching a photograph I had ripped out of a magazine, my mum tactfully trying to explain to me that my hair wouldn't go like that.

When I was about nine, a particular hairdresser who clearly had never touched afro hair before, ended up cutting most of it off. I was devastated. I remember seeing the hairdresser a few weeks later at the beach. She smiled and waved at my mum. Tears welled up inside of me. I was so angry with her. Did she not realize what she had done?

When I was growing up, other than my mum, there was never another white person who defended me. It was painful; it made me anxious, and at times I questioned my own sanity.

I went to a white majority school. It was also an all-girls school, which brought another dynamic – lots of teenagers trying to find their place in the hierarchy. Gossip, friendship break-ups, and navigating popularity, but race relations added another complication.

When I was eleven, a girl shoved past me to get to the paints in an art lesson. She was the kind of character who seemed to be able to do and say whatever she wanted with very little consequence. I shot her a dirty look and she turned to me and whispered, "You ni**er."

I was shocked and also had no idea what to do. If I told the other girls I couldn't be sure anyone would stick up for me. I looked over at Mrs Peerless, our art teacher, who was probably in her sixties. She had a grey bowl cut, white overcoat, and glasses that sat at the end of her nose. She had a kind face. I decided she was my only hope. At least she would issue a detention or call the girl's parents.

> **TELLING SOMEONE WHO HAD JUST BEEN CALLED A RACIST INSULT THAT "WE ARE THE SAME" IS TO IGNORE THEIR VERY REAL EXPERIENCE AND DISMISS THEIR VALID EMOTIONS.**

I took a deep breath and walked over to her. She ushered me into the corner of the studio and I explained what happened. Before I'd finished she shouted across the room and called the other student over. And as expected, she talked her way out of it. She said I misheard and she had called me a "piggler". The teacher looked at us both and loudly said for the class to hear, "We're all the same." That was the end of the matter. Well, it probably was for them.

Maybe the teacher thought she was doing the right thing at the time. I used to hear the "we're all the same" argument a lot. While we know race is a social construct, we also know that we are not all treated the same and we do not all have equal opportunities. Telling someone who had just been called a racist insult that "we are the same" is to ignore their very real experience and dismiss their valid emotions.

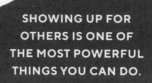

SHOWING UP FOR OTHERS IS ONE OF THE MOST POWERFUL THINGS YOU CAN DO.

At that moment my teacher should have been my ally. She should have taken the load off me and advocated on my behalf. At the very least, she should have spoken to that student about how violent that word is and checked in with me after the incident to see if I was okay. It's only on reflection, and now that I am a teacher myself, that I understand how badly she failed me.

Now, twenty-five years after this incident and many others, I understand it's not me with the problem. The lack of understanding about racism isn't my responsibility and I don't need to try and fit in with white people's expectations of me. The more we as BIPOC (Black, Indigenous, People of Colour) or those who call ourselves allies challenge racism when we see and hear it, the less power it has. Showing up for others is one of the most powerful things you can do.

Allies would have supported the train conductor and Natalie that day. They would have stopped Natalie from being the only person to say something publicly. I wouldn't have needed to be the "shoulder to cry on", to relive the past trauma and painful memories we have endured throughout our life.

Allyship can show up in all different forms; however, in this case, we are talking about being a public ally. Racism needs to be challenged when it's seen or heard and not just by those who it's directed at. Silence is dangerous. It can imply you are complicit and in agreement with what is being said. So what makes people not do anything when they see racism?

A potential answer lies in the bystander effect or bystander apathy, a social psychological theory which states that the greater the number of people present in a situation, the less likely they are to intervene. It's also known as diffusion of responsibility. The more onlookers there are, the less personal accountability individuals will feel to take action. In short, everyone assumes someone else will speak out, so they don't have to. It would be a lie to say it's easy to speak up when someone is being racist.

It can be a daunting prospect, but one thing I have learnt is that it only takes one person to make a difference.

NATALIE

Months had passed since the incident on the train. I had shown a few of my friends the video. Most of my friends are white and their responses are usually the same: "I can't believe it" and "I am so sorry." When I showed my Black friends, I warned them it was triggering. One of my friends told me I needed to put it online so he could share the video to his large Twitter following. I declined. I was still embarrassed by the way I handled things and I couldn't bear to see negative comments from online trolls.

A few weeks went by and the murder of Ahmaud Arbery happened in America. He was a Black man lynched by two white men while he was out running. They had taken it upon themselves to follow Ahmaud and shoot him dead in broad daylight in the street while an observer filmed the murder.

I was in my car waiting for my sister to come out of the supermarket when I first saw the video. I cried and cried, my stomach sick. As I looked online I saw the same comments I have heard my whole life: "I can't believe this is happening", "How does racism still exist?", and "So glad this doesn't happen in the UK." Some of these comments were coming from some of my closest friends and family. Did they really think this? Are people so naive that they believe racism doesn't exist here in the UK?

By the time I got home I had made up my mind. I told Naomi we needed to post the video of the train incident. I wanted people to see that racism was happening in the UK and to understand what we have to put up with nearly every day, whether it's directed at us or not. Naomi agreed. We both knew it was the right time.

I WANTED PEOPLE TO SEE THAT RACISM WAS HAPPENING IN THE UK AND TO UNDERSTAND WHAT WE HAVE TO PUT UP WITH NEARLY EVERY DAY . . .

We discussed the consequences of people outside our circle seeing the video and the abusive things that might be said, but we were fed up with having the same conversations with each other. As I uploaded the video, my stomach felt queasy and my heart was thumping, like I felt when I was on the train. I clicked upload and from that moment our lives would change forever and in ways we would never have imagined.

Millions of people have now watched that incident. The video went viral, and as we watched it being shared all over social media Naomi looked at me and said, "We need to do more." The next day we started Everyday Racism, a safe space on social media for BIPOC in the UK to share their stories about everyday racist encounters.

When you have experienced a racist incident, one of the most difficult things is worrying about how people will respond when you speak up. You can be interrogated, accused of being too sensitive or overreacting – even if you are telling the truth.

To this day, there are many people who think racism is a thing of the past, and we want to make sure people can share their own accounts honestly and in their own words, so others don't feel alone. We now have followers from all over the world and we also share resources about how to be an effective ally in everyday life, as well as information to educate people on issues around racism.

You see, telling your story is a powerful way to be an ally and to help others become allies, too. You never know who it can impact and the lasting change it can have.

ACKNOWLEDGEMENTS

SHAKIRAH:
We couldn't have done this project without Super-Agent Marietta B. Zacker, who brought us together, and advised, guided, commiserated, and ultimately added her own amazing words.

DANA:
And big thanks to the entire DK team, especially Tori Kosara, who juggled a million flaming chainsaws, and Anne Sharples, and the rest of the super-talented art, editorial, and marketing teams.

SHAKIRAH:
And don't forget fairies like Ayesha Gibson-Gill, Lisa Stringfellow, Lisa Springer, and Lloyda Garrett. Thank you to all of our family and friends who supported us with words of encouragement and advice. We love you!

DANA:
And most importantly, this project would never exist without the incredible talent and grace of the authors who trusted us with their stories. Thank you for your patience with us as we learnt to be editors.

SHAKIRAH:
And cake. We can't forget cake and all your cats.

DANA:
And a final heartfelt thanks to Shakirah, my sister-from-another-mister, without whom I would have given up on this project and run into the sea months ago.

SHAKIRAH:
#DakirahForever

Penguin
Random
House

Senior Editor Tori Kosara
Editorial Assistant Nicole Reynolds
Senior Art Editors David McDonald and Anne Sharples
Designer Anita Mangan
Production Editor Siu Yin Chan
Senior Production Editor Jennifer Murray
Senior Production Controllers Louise Minihane and
Lloyd Robertson
Managing Editor Paula Regan
Managing Art Editor Jo Connor
Publishing Director Mark Searle

DK would like to thank the editors, Shakirah Bourne
and Dana Alison Levy; the authors, Marietta B. Zacker
at Gallt & Zacker Literary Agency; Lavinya Stennett and
the team at The Black Curriculum; and Bianca Hezekiah
for authenticity review. Also, at DK, Julia March for Anglicising;
Anne Damerell, Nicola Evans, Emily Kimball, Grace Nyaboko, and
Nishani Reed; Ruth Amos for editorial help; and the DK Diversity,
Equity & Inclusion team, in particular the Product and Content
Working Group and Lisa Gillespie for their insight and guidance.

To Marietta,
thanks for wearing all the hats.

To everyone reading,
thank you for taking this journey with us.

— Shakirah and Dana

WORLD BOOK DAY
2 MARCH 2023

HAPPY
WORLD BOOK DAY!

Choosing to read in your spare time can make you happier and more successful. We want that for every young person.

NOW YOU'VE READ THIS BOOK YOU COULD:

• Swap it • Read it again • Recommend it to a friend • Talk about it

WHERE WILL YOUR READING JOURNEY
TAKE YOU NEXT?

Why not challenge a friend, teacher, local bookseller or librarian
to recommend your next read based on your interests?

START A BOOK RECOMMENDATION CHAT!

• I really liked... so what could I read next?
• I like books that have... these characters, plots, or information
• I've never tried this type of genre... e.g. non-fiction, poetry, crime

...can you recommend a good place to start?

WORLD BOOK DAY
2 MARCH 2023

WHERE CAN YOU FIND YOUR NEXT READ? YOU CAN...

1 TAKE A TRIP TO YOUR LOCAL BOOKSHOP

2 JOIN YOUR LOCAL LIBRARY

3 CHECK OUT THE WORLD BOOK DAY WEBSITE

NATALIE AND NAOMI OFFER SOME GREAT ANTI-RACISM ADVICE

Natalie and Naomi Evans are the founders of Everyday Racism, a platform dedicated to sharing anti-racism resources and testimonies from BIPOC. Be a part of the anti-racism movement on Instagram @everydayracism_

HOW TO AVOID THE BYSTANDER EFFECT

What contributes to the bystander effect?

- Conscious and unconscious bias
- Being fearful
- Believing it's not your responsibility
- Thinking someone else will step in
- Remaining unaware
- Prejudice and discrimination

HOW TO BECOME AN ACTIVE BYSTANDER

- Learn how to become a better ally: read, listen to podcasts, and watch programmes.
- Address your conscious and unconscious bias.
- Learn the language to interrupt the situation and educate yourself.
- Remind yourself that this is your responsibility.
- Remember, when you intervene it can also encourage others to step up.